African Americans in Michigan

DISCOVERING THE PEOPLES OF MICHIGAN
Arthur W. Helweg and Linwood H. Cousins, Series Editors

Ethnicity in Michigan: Issues and People
Jack Glazier, Arthur W. Helweg

French Canadians in Michigan
John P. DuLong

African Americans in Michigan
Lewis Walker, Benjamin C. Wilson, Linwood H. Cousins

Albanians in Michigan
Frances Trix

———————————

Discovering the Peoples of Michigan is a series of publications examining the state's rich multicultural heritage. The series makes available an interesting, affordable, and varied collection of books that enables students and lay readers to explore Michigan's ethnic dynamics. A knowledge of the state's rapidly changing multicultural history has far-reaching implications for human relations, education, public policy, and planning. We believe that *Discovering the Peoples of Michigan* will enhance understanding of the unique contributions that diverse and often unrecognized communities have made to Michigan's history and culture.

African Americans in Michigan

Lewis Walker
Benjamin C. Wilson
Linwood H. Cousins

Michigan State University Press

East Lansing

♾ The paper used in this publication meets the minimum requirements
of ANSI/NISO Z39.48-1992 (R 1997) (Permanence of Paper)

Michigan State University Press
East Lansing, Michigan 48823-5202
Printed and bound in the United States of America

05 04 03 02 01   1 2 3 4 5 6 7 8 9

LIBRARY OF CONGRESS CATALOGING-IN-PUBLICATION DATA
library of congress cataloging-in-publication data

Walker, Lewis, 1922–
African Americans in Michigan / Lewis Walker, Benjamin C. Wilson, Linwood H. Cousins.
p. cm. — (Discovering the peoples of Michigan)
Includes bibliographical references (p.   ) and index.
ISBN 0-87013-583-X (paper : alk. paper)
1. African Americans—Michigan—History. 2. African Americans—Education—Michigan—History.
3. Michigan—History. I. Wilson, Benjamin C. II. Cousins, Linwood H., 1955– III. Title. IV. Series.
E185.93.M5 W35 2001
977.4'00496073—dc21
2001000319

Discovering the Peoples of Michigan. The editors wish to thank the Kellogg
Foundation for their generous support. Special thanks goes to the Department
of Black Americana at Western Michigan University and the Lewis Walker
Institute for Race and Ethnic Relations for their support of this volume.

Cover design by Ariana Grabec-Dingman
Book design by Sharp Des!gns, Inc.

The photographs and freed papers that appear in this volume are courtesy
of the Ben C. Wilson Collection in the Department of Black Americana Studies
at Western Michigan University; additional photos courtesy
of Linwood H. Cousins.

Visit Michigan State University Press on the World Wide Web at:
www.msupress.msu.edu

*To my mother, Mrs. Thelma Freeman, and my
late mother-in-law, Mrs. Gussie A. Doles.*

LEWIS WALKER

*This book is dedicated to my biological mother, Ms. Winifred
J. Wilson, and my ex-mother-in-law, Ms. Bertha Coates Graves,
who will remain in my daughters' and my lives forever.*

BEN C. WILSON

*This volume is dedicated to Drs. Lewis Walker and Benjamin
Wilson, whose scholarship has focused on the historical recovery
of African American life in Michigan. Though Walker has recently
retired, he and Wilson have been long-term, well-known professors at Western Michigan University in Kalamazoo, where they
have spent most of their careers in Sociology and Black Africana
Studies, respectively. These professors have dedicated their academic lives to documenting and disseminating information
about African Americans in Michigan, which includes the role of
Michigan in the Underground Railroad, African American life in
rural southwestern Michigan and urban Detroit, and the once
idyllic resort African Americans frequented in Idlewild, Michigan.*

LINWOOD H. COUSINS

SERIES ACKNOWLEDGMENTS

Discovering the Peoples of Michigan is a series of publications that resulted from the cooperation and effort of many individuals. The people recognized here are not a complete representation, for the list of contributors is too numerous to mention. However, credit must be given to Jeffrey Bonevich, who worked tirelessly with me on contacting people as well as researching and organizing material. He read and reread, checked and rechecked, and continually kept in contact with contributors.

The initial idea for this project came from Mary Erwin, but I must thank Fred Bohm, director of the Michigan State University Press, for seeing the need for this project, for giving it his strong support, and for making publication possible. Also, the tireless efforts of Keith Widder and Elizabeth Demers, senior editors at Michigan State University Press, were vital in bringing DPOM to fruition. Keith put his heart and soul into this series, and his dedication was instrumental in its success.

Otto Feinstein and Germaine Strobel of the Michigan Ethnic Heritage Studies Center patiently and willingly provided names for contributors and constantly gave this project their tireless support.

My late wife, Usha Mehta Helweg, was the initial editor. She meticulously went over manuscripts. Her suggestions and advice were crucial. Initial typing, editing, and formatting were also done by Majda Seuss, Priya Helweg, and Carol Nickolai.

The maps were drawn by Fritz Seegers while the graphics showing ethnic residential patterns in Michigan were done by the Geographical Information Center (GIS) at Western Michigan University under the directorship of David Dickason.

Russell Magnaghi must also be given special recognition for his willingness to do much more than be a contributor. He provided author contacts as well as information to the series' writers. Other authors and organizations provided comments on other aspects of the work. There are many people that were interviewed by the various authors who will remain anonymous. However, they have enabled the story of their group to be told. Unfortunately, their names are not available, but we are grateful for their cooperation.

Most of all, this work is a tribute to the writers who patiently gave their time to write and share their research findings. Their contributions are noted and appreciated. To them goes most of the gratitude.

Arthur W. Helweg

Series Co-Editor

Contents

Introduction, *Linwood H. Cousins and Arthur W. Helweg* 1

African Americans in Michigan, *Lewis Walker*
   and Benjamin C. Wilson 3
  Underground Railroad Routes 8
  Freed Papers 13

Ethnicity in Identity Politics in the Schooling Experiences of African
American High School Students, *Linwood H. Cousins* 31
  Detroit Public Schools 33

Notes 49

For Further Reference 55

Index 61

Discovering the Peoples of Michigan: Introduction to African Americans in Michigan

Linwood H. Cousins and Arthur W. Helweg

While doing graduate work at the University of Michigan in Ann Arbor, one of the editors, Linwood H. Cousins, became friends with a visiting scholar from Switzerland. Cousins found his friend, François, to be relatively open minded and well-read. So, as they discussed François's knowledge and awareness of African Americans, Cousins was surprised to learn that his friend's view of this ethnic group was based on distorted, shamefully inaccurate portrayals. As have many other people outside the United States, François came to believe that African Americans no longer labored under the vestiges of slavery. In other words, he thought the forces of racism had dissipated because of the civil rights movement and the U.S. propaganda broadcast abroad about equality for all. What he had learned from media and other sources of information in Switzerland and Europe in general was that the kind of inequality African Americans face in housing, schooling, and economic opportunities did not exist. Indeed, he believed that American prosperity was being equally shared by all. Over the next few months and years Cousins and François undertook many discussions and activities and they began by examining the experiences of African Americans in Michigan.

In the first article in this volume, Lewis Walker and Benjamin Wilson
document how African American people in Michigan made numerous
contributions to the state, but never outside the bondage of slavery or
the unrelenting oppression of racism. Certainly many other histories of
African Americans in the state remain to be told. Walker and Wilson
could have written the history of Idlewild, an African American resort
that was popular between 1912 and the 1960s. Or they could have
described the rise and fall of Benton Harbor, an African American community in Michigan. These histories may yet be written. But for now,
the authors provide the foundation for explorations in Michigan's
African American history.

In the second part of the volume, Linwood Cousins explores the
issue of education alluded to in Walker and Wilson's article. Cousins
takes his understanding of the historical centrality of education in the
African American struggle for freedom and equality, and extends it into
contemporary ethnic, racial, and class relations in the schools.

Cousins uses the example of a Newark, New Jersey school as a back-
drop for the ethnic and racial identity politics faced by African
Americans in Michigan schools. He focuses on the peculiar ways in
which systematic historical and contemporary relations of race, ethnicity, and class—also described by Walker and Wilson—exact similar
outcomes for African Americans in Michigan and other states across
the United States.

What's more, Cousins has spent more than a decade in Michigan living and working with African Americans, and studying black history and
culture in rural and urban contexts. Regardless of statewide differences
that flow from African Americans' ethnic, racial, and class relations,
commonalities exist that allow for the discovery of African Americans'
unique history in Michigan and its broader links with U.S. history.

The purpose of the *Discovering the Peoples of Michigan* series is not
limited to setting forth the experiences and contributions of Michigan's
various population segments, but to understand better and deal with
the rapid ethnic diversification that is taking place in the state.
Knowledge of Michigan's diverse population will help illuminate multicultural, pluralistic, and ethnic issues that are rapidly developing in
Michigan and the United States.

African Americans in Michigan

Lewis Walker and Benjamin C. Wilson

Although slavery was abolished in the United States more than 135 years ago, an understanding of the development of the rural and urban black American communities cannot be fully understood without some acquaintance of slavery history. The history of blacks in Michigan and elsewhere in the country began in a colonial context, dating back to the expansion of Europe during the fifteenth and sixteenth centuries. At present, blacks live in a context of neocolonialism because, although marked progress has been made, poverty and racism still persist in economically depressed industrial cities and rural areas.

Edna Bonacich succinctly outlines this historical development in the following statement:[1]

> The Europeans managed to convince themselves that their reign of terror was really beneficent, bringing enlightenment, religion, and economic development to the savages. In fact, they often brought genocide and enslavement. The plunder they took helped to build the economic and military might of Europe. . . . Africans were forcibly brought to the Americas for one reason: so that white property owners could exploit their labor for profit. . . . In our view, the United States continues to be a deeply racist society despite this rhetoric. Racism continues to remain

here in at least two aspects of the system. First, it consists in the continued exploitation of people of color for profit. And second, it is demonstrated in the demand that people of color must accommodate to the white man's system, rather than vice versa.

In 1997, according to the Bureau of Census's projections, a total of 1,358,586 black Americans resided in Michigan, or 13.9 percent of the state's 9,774,000 total population. This proportion has remained constant over the last ten to fifteen years. Regarding Michigan's eighty-three counties, black Americans are found in relatively small numbers in areas north of the lower-tier counties. Michigan's current black population did not, however, suddenly appear overnight; it has an interesting, albeit tortuous, history.

Antebellum Migration Period

The ancestors of Michigan's blacks came in chains largely from Africa's West Coast. Between 8,000,000 and 10,0000,000 Africans were brought to South America between 1510 and 1880, and there were approximately 4,000,000 blacks in the United States in 1861.[2]

Slavery in the United States was a peculiar institution more nearly perfected in all of its complexities and ugliness in the southern region of the country. Michigan, on the other hand, flirted with slavery, but it never reached the same magnitude as in Kentucky, Virginia, Mississippi, Alabama, South Carolina or North Carolina. Far from being a state where slavery developed into a flourishing economic institution, Michigan was at the center of antislavery agitation once it became a state in 1837. The state became an integral and vital part of the Underground Railroad, which gave passage to an unknown number of fugitive slaves traveling to Canada and other safe havens. Nevertheless, there were a few slaves living in the territory, mainly in the Detroit and Michilimakinac areas.

David Katzman, in a seminal piece on black slavery in Michigan, characterizes the slave experience in Michigan as consisting of a negligible number of black bondsmen; their life experiences were far less brutal and degrading than their counterparts in the southern states.

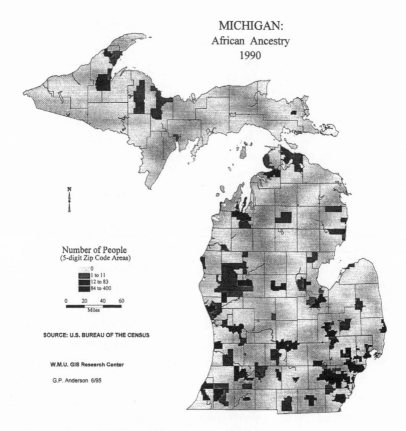

Figure 1. Map of Michigan African Ancestry (1990).

In taking on a slave, the lone voyageur probably sought companionship as well as additional labor. The slave thus became something other than a slave, perhaps a servant, possibly a companion. As was true of the *voyageurs*, few slaves ever became traders, although many rose to the rank of interpreters or subordinate traders on a salary. In any event, the frontier slave of northern Michigan and the surrounding areas escaped the curse of self-deprecation and despair that stigmatized the Southern plantation slave.[3]

According to the federal census, there were twenty-four slaves in the Michigan territory in 1810, none in 1820, and thirty-two in 1830. Before

Michigan's entry into the Union as a free state in 1837, "there were three slaves in Michigan—two in Monroe County and one in Cass County."[4] During the antebellum years, southern-born white Quakers facilitated the increase of Michigan's black population. As early as 1812, approximately 5,000 to 7,000 members of that sect migrated north and by 1843 there were roughly 7,000 to 10,000 Quakers in the state; many were concentrated in Cass County. As a result of the Quakers' presence, the availability of uncultivated land, and the remoteness of the area, there developed viable black communities in Cass County, including many prosperous black farmers. The Quaker presence was felt in almost every city, village, and hamlet between Berrien and Wayne Counties. Regardless of where they built their homes, most of the Quakers, especially the more radical Hicksites, became and remained implacable foes of the "peculiar institution." Some were so conscientious that they refused to use goods produced by slave labor. The Hicksites, however, were not the only religious people who refrained from using products associated with "slavocracy." For example, the Reverend Luther Humphrey, a Cass County Baptist minister, neither ate nor used anything made in the South. As a substitute for sugar, he used juice extracted from corn to make his own unique blend of syrup.

Some of the most active Quakers, who risked life and property for the cause, included: E. McIlvain and L. P. Alexander (Niles); Stephen Bogue, Zacharian Shugart, Ishmael Lee, Josiah Osborn (Cass County); Dr. Nathan Macy Thomas (Schoolcraft); Dr. William Wheeler (Flowerfield); Henry Montague (Oshtemo); Orrin Snow (Kalamazoo); Erastus Hussey, Silas Dodge, August Rawson, John Caldwell, Abel Densmore, Henry Willis, Theron Chadwick Sr., S. B. Thayer, Charles Barnes, Henry J. Cushman, Charles Wheelers, Drs. Cox and Campbell, Dr. E. A. Atlee, Samuel Strauther, Samuel Nicholas, Thomas Henderson, William McCullon, and others (Calhoun County); Townsend E. Gidley (Parma); Lonson Wilcox and Normal Allen (Jackson); Samuel W. Dexter (Dexter); Theodore Foster (Scio); Guy Beckley (Ann Arbor); and John Geddes (Geddes). Once the runaways reached Detroit, nearly every black settler's residence was a "safe house," but some homes like those of William Webb, William Lambert, and George DeBaptiste, were readily available. Without question, the work of white Detroiter Seymour

Finney, who worked valiantly with others to increase the number of sanctuaries for black fugitives, deserves special recognition.

The Quaker and black abolitionists moved passengers on the primary routes that ran from Toledo to Detroit, Toledo to Adrian to Detroit, St. Joseph to Detroit, Chicago to Detroit, Muskegon to Detroit, Detroit to Saginaw, and Chicago to the Upper Peninsula. Detroit was important because it was one of the major entry points to Canada. Usually the passwords for the freedom train were: "Can you give shelter and protection to one or more person?" The following is an example of a cryptic message sent from one agent to another: "By tomorrow evening you will receive two volumes of the irrepressible conflict bound in black. After perusal, please forward and oblige." In addition to these code words, there were nonverbal signals such as the broad brim black hat, the conspicuous presence of a drinking gourd near the door, the ladies attired in the long black dresses with matching bonnets, hand signals, men with full beards and no mustaches, etc. It was common practice for the Underground Railroad stations to be no more than fifteen to twenty miles apart, and not surprisingly, most of the conductors knew very little about their colleagues. In Michigan, because of the state's distance from the slave states, moving the runaways usually took place in broad daylight. The majority of the runaways from the upper south (Kentucky, Maryland, Delaware, and Virginia), however, traveled under the cover of darkness.

The experiences of fugitives and Underground Railroad operatives were vividly portrayed in family lore, novels, biographies, news clippings, and songs. An old slave song, one of the most authentic to be handed down from pre–Civil War plantation days, recounts the risks that slaves took in escaping from bondage:

RUN, NIGGER, RUN

Run, nigger, run; de patter-roller catch you;
Run, nigger, run; it's almost day.
Run, nigger, run; de patter-roller catch you;
Run, nigger, run, and try to get away.
Dis nigger run, he run his best,
Stuck his head in a hornet's nest,

Underground Railroad Routes

Route One: Toledo to Detroit

This ran along the waterways of Lake Erie, the Detroit River, Lake St. Clair and the St. Clair River. George DeBaptiste was the most famous operator along this route.

Route Two: Toledo to Adrian to Detroit

This follows a trail that began in Toledo and ran into Monroe County and eventually into Lenawee County. Then it went through Tecumseh, the lower quadrant of Washtenaw County and on to Detroit. The principal operatives were Laura Haviland and Prior Foster of Adrian.

Route Three: St. Joseph to Detroit

This route was the Old Sauk Trail that entered Michigan from Indiana along the Lake Michigan shoreline and ran through St. Joseph, Branch and Hillsdale Counties, and on to Detroit. The most important conductors were: John Zimmerman of Union City, John G. Parkhurst of Coldwater, Theodore Foster of Scio (now a ghost town), Seymour Treadwell of the Jackson area, and Gamalia Bailey of Manchester.

Route Four: Chicago to Detroit

This covers roughly the counties running along the old Territorial Road from Chicago to Detroit. Among the towns where underground operators worked were Niles, Vandalia, Schoolcraft, Kalamazoo, Battle Creek, Marshall, and Jackson. This route was also called the Quaker Route or the Michigan Central Line. A few of the well known operators were E. McIlvain and L. P. Alexander of Niles; Zachariah Shugart, Ishmael Lee, Josiah Osburn of Vandalia and Cassopolis; William Wheeler of Flowerfield; Dr. Nathan Macy Thomas of Schoolcraft; Henry Montague of Oshtemo; Orrin Snow of Kalamazoo; Benjamin Fox of Yorkville; Dr. Uriah Upjohn and Deacon Simeon Mills of Richland; the Mays families of Gull Prairie; Isaac Davis of Climax; Erastus Hussey, Samuel Strawther, Silas Dodge, August Rawson John Caldwell, Abel Densmore, Henry Willis, Theron H. Chadwick, Dr. S. B. Thayer, Charles Barnes, Henry J. Crushman et al. of the Battle Creek area.

Route Five: Muskegon

This followed the Grand River Valley from Lake Michigan to Jackson and included stations in Muskegon, Grand Rapids, Lansing, and other places. Runaways were ferried east and west along the routes as well as along tributaries leading to the Grand River. Ira Maxfield and Mayfield in the small village of Lamont and Aaron Ingersoll in the village of Leslie were active operators. The Collins A. M. E. Church was a vital resting spot for the fugitives in Lansing.

Route Six: Detroit to Saginaw Bay

This ran from the outskirts of Detroit to Saginaw and the Bay area. This was an alternate route leading away from heavily used Detroit stations into Canada, specifically Ontario, Quebec, and Nova Scotia. Nathan Powers and his family in Farmington were the best known operatives.

Route Seven: Chicago to the Upper Peninsula

This trail ran along Lake Michigan's eastern shoreline from Chicago through the Upper Peninsula. Frequently boats were used. Walter Duke, an African American boatman, transported many fugitives. (Quite a few runaway slaves played a vital role in the growth and development of the Emmet County ghost town—Freedom.)

> Jumped de fence and run fru de paster,
> White man run, but nigger run faster.
>
> —*From the Benjamin C. Wilson Collection, Western Michigan University.*

Reminiscing about some of his exploits, Battle Creek's Erastus Hussey told an interesting story:

> A slave woman who had been here about a week was assisting my wife with her work when a party of slaves drove up. Among the number was her daughter whom she had not seen in 10 years. The recognition was mutual and the meeting a very affecting sight. . . . One day a fugitive and his wife came to my house for shelter. He had been a slave of Wade

Hampton (South Carolina), and some called him by that name. Hampton worked about here for three days. One day while we were at dinner, Jim Logan came walking in. The colored woman gave a shriek, jumped up from the table and almost fainted. . . . She and Jim had been engaged to be married in Kentucky; not having heard from him in two years she had married Wade Hampton.[5]

Arrival in Michigan did not mean, by any stretch of the imagination, that the fugitives were safe. On numerous occasions Michigan whites were steadfast in their fight against "slave raiders" who ventured into Michigan to return runaways to "their owners." Levi Coffin, in his reminiscences, relates his experience with Reverend A. Stevens, who came into Michigan with a group of raiders to "fetch" his property. When word spread that Stevens and his raiders were already busy in the area taking runaways into custody, the whites destroyed his wagon, sank it in Birch Lake, and captured him. He was forced to dismount his horse so a black mother could ride, and

whenever they passed a house, the people were called out to look at that child-stealer, a preacher. When they reach . . . [settlements] in the county. . . . Bill Jones further compelled him to march up and down the street[s] and called the attention of the people to this divine who had been stealing a negro [sic] babe and taunted him so much that he actually cried with vexation.[6]

They came—the Julia Washingtons, the Frances Johnsons, the Peter Tones, the William Coles, the Mary Mills, the Albert Wilsons, the John Wesleys, the Abraham Lanes, the James Grifens, the Robert Bradleys, and countless others—all runaway slaves, to Michigan to escape the bitter harshness of slavery. They were men, women, and children determined to throw off the shackles of slavery and live their lives in the dignity of freedom, not the degradation of slavery.

As one might suspect, runaway slaves did not constitute the majority of black settlers in the state during the pre–Civil War Years. One can guess that fugitives accounted for roughly five percent of the total black population, or less than 350 people. Free and quasi-freed blacks, then,

Figure 2. Mr. Henry Clark and his family of Battle Creek: The Clark family descended from Thomas Clark, the son of a slave owner who settled in Battle Creek (From the Benjamin C. Wilson Collection. Black American Studies Department. Western Michigan University).

contributed more substantially to the state's population growth. Many quasi-freed blacks were sent or brought north by masters who were also their fathers.

Thomas Clark, the slave and son of Obitida Clark (a slave owner), and a fugitive female slave settled in Battle Creek after a temporary stay in Cabin Creek, Indiana. Of the quasi-freed blacks who came to Michigan, the Thomas Clark case is a most interesting one because he

> grew up with his half-brother, John. While John went to school, Thomas worked. When their father died, Thomas was willed to his half-brother. He became John's personal servant. John wanted Thomas to be free. They decided to go north where Thomas could work for his freedom. In 1837, they boarded a train for Indiana. Blacks had a special section in which to ride but John let Thomas sit beside him. His skin was light and he could easily pass. But just to make sure he wasn't taken for a slave, John gave him a newspaper and told him to pretend he was reading it. . . . Thomas held the newspaper but it wasn't until they arrived at Cabin Creek, Indiana

*Figure 3. Mary Lewis King and her Husband (1866): Slaves masters who were
fathers of slave children sometimes felt responsible for their mulatto children.
Many freed them and purchased land for them in a free state. Cass, Berrien, and
Van Buren counties were areas in Michigan chosen by some slave fathers. The
father of Mary Lewis King decided on Arlington Township in Van Buren County.
Later, she married Alfred King in Paw Paw on 26 September 1866. Husband and
wife appear in this early photo (From the Benjamin C. Wilson Collection. Black
American Studies Department. Western Michigan University).*

that it was discovered he had been holding it upside down. . . . Thomas
was finally able to pay his half brother for his freedom. The price was
$5,000. He was now free and so was his young son, Henry . . . he loved
showing people his freedom papers. . . . By 1861 blacks, even those who
were free, were having trouble dodging slavehunters. Men came from the
South looking for slaves as far north as Indiana and even into Michigan.
Perhaps that's why three of Thomas Clark's children were sent to Battle
Creek. They were welcomed in Battle Creek.[7]

The children of slaveholders were preceded by large migrations of
legally freed blacks from neighboring northern states, especially Ohio
and Indiana. A densely populated valley, bordering the Greenville
Creek, which extended from southwest Ohio to southeast Ohio and
portions of central Indiana, also contributed heavily to the black

Freed Papers

The following is a copy of a portion of a "Freed Paper," in its entirety, issued to Jack James, whose ancestors eventually settled in Calvin Township in Cass County, Michigan. In antebellum America this document always had to be carried by its owner, whether in the north or in the south.

State of North Carolina, Wake County

I, Benjamin S. King [,] clerk of the Court of Pleas and Quarter Sessions for the County of Wake aforesaid do hereby certify that Charlotte G. Rhodes who signed her name to the above certificate is a lady of respectability who verasity cannot be doubted. I further certify that Jack James, the above named free man of colour, came personally before me this day and produced his two sons and one daughter with his wife (to-wit) Ervin, Jesse and Lang James. Jack James is round built about five-feet five inches high [,] has a scar on his brest in the centre [,] dark mulato coloured and about fifty-seven years of age—Earvin [,] his son about five feet seven inches high, a little lighter than his father, has a remarkable finger on his left hand, the four finger from having been cut at the end makes it appear as if two nails were on one finger, a large and small one, he is about twenty years old. Jesse James the youngest son is a light mulatoe about five-feet four inches high rather, slender built and about seventeen years of age.

Jack James' wife is nearly white, rather of the Indian appearance, slender built and about forty years old [.] She has been a resident of this county for many years [,] they are regularly married as I understand. I have never heard it doubted but they are all free persons of colour. Lang James is about the colour of her mother, rather dusky, is about fourteen years of age. This family of free person of colour say they are about to remove somewhere to the west, and request this certificate of men. I have personal knowledge of Jack James. I have found him to be an orderly man and I think I can say that the whole family are respectable in their situation in life as free colored persons and therefore think that wherever they may go that they ought to be respected as such.

In testimony whereof I have hereto set may hand and the seal of office at Raleigh this 11th day of November, A.D. 1831.

(Signed) B. S. King, Clerk

—From the Benjamin C. Wilson Collection, Western Michigan University.

population growth of antebellum Michigan. Due to overcrowding and increasing racial hostility (expressed in anti-free black laws) in those Ohio and Indiana areas, many blacks found living conditions unbearable, so they decided to follow their Quaker friends to Michigan.

Between 1840 and 1865, the freed blacks who migrated to the state from the Ohio side of the Greenville Valley came primarily from Logan, Mercer, Drake, and Shelby Counties; from the Indiana side of the valley freed blacks came from either Randolph, Shelby, or Wayne Counties. The trips from Ohio and Indiana, although fraught with drudgery and unanticipated hardships, did not have the drama or the danger encountered by the fugitive slaves, especially those attempting an escape from the South. John J. Evans, who eventually settled in Battle Creek, gives an account of such a trip:

> In 1854 Evan's father, imbued with the belief that the north presented better advantages for the success of his family than did the slave states, . . . came to Indiana. This was the time when refugee colored families were hunted down by owners, and Indiana was a most convenient state for these repeated raids.[8]
>
> Fearing for the safety of his family, he arranged to bring them further north, when death overtook him. . . . The mother's indomitable will, however, was guided by her late husband's counsel and she concluded to carry out the idea of getting the family further north, so she started for Cass County, Michigan. Not liking the surroundings there, she came to this city (Battle Creek), the whole journey from the south being completed during the year.

In 1847 Sampson Saunders from Cabell County, Virginia (now West Virginia), viewed slavery as a repulsive institution. At age thirty, he inherited an estate from a deceased uncle that included seventeen slaves—ten men, five women, and two minors. Wanting to free his slaves without leaving them destitute, Saunders considered purchasing land in the neighborhood for their settlement, setting aside part of his plantation, or transporting them to Africa where the American Colonization Society had set up a "dumping ground" in Liberia for America's unwanted freed black population. He thought, too, of the possibility of sending them to a Caribbean Island—Santo Domingo, Haiti, Jamaica, or Bermuda. None of his plans proved feasible. After three years of searching, undaunted still in his determination that none of "his" blacks would ever toil in another southern field, he chose Michigan.[9]

Postbellum Migration Period

The end of the Civil War did not signal the end of black migration to Michigan. From the postbellum years to the post–World War II period, the trickle of blacks into the state slowly became a deluge, especially to certain counties and cities. An increase in black migration, however, exacerbated the ever-present debate over "colored suffrage." (An organization of black and white agitators had unsuccessfully pursued the right to vote issues in the early 1850s.) Widespread "negrophobia" over this and other issues was the reason that "many whites regarded the existence of a colored population as unfortunate, wished it would go away, and fervently hoped it would not multiply."[10] Blacks, however, were allowed to vote in school elections as far back as 1855, but "blacks were disenfranchised in Michigan until the 15th Amendment nullified the Michigan constitution's ban on black suffrage in 1870."[11]

During the period of southern Reconstruction (1866–77), many blacks were enticed to move to Michigan by such notables as Sojourner Truth. After the passage of the 13th, 14th, and 15th Amendments few former fugitives who had opted to settle in the province of Ontario (Cresden, Sarnia, and other rural areas in Canada near the Michigan border) were attracted to Michigan's available land in the central portion of the state. The Berrys, the Bracys, the Owens, and others migrated to Mecosta, Montcalm, Genesee, and Isabella Counties.

Thomas Cross was one of many who came because he could purchase forty acres of inexpensive virgin land for the price of a healthy horse. Some, such as the Letts, settled in Ingham or Manistee County. Between 1866 and 1910, the black population of southwest Michigan experienced some growth, especially in those counties that already had settled and well-established African American communities.

Numerous factors accounted for this gradual increase in population size. For the towns, especially Kalamazoo and Battle Creek, employment opportunities in service work or skilled crafts attracted those who were not devoted to agricultural labor. The number of black inhabitants in Kalamazoo grew gradually, from 361 in 1870 to 471 in 1900. By 1910 there were 790 black residents in Kalamazoo County and 685 in the city. The number fluctuated in Battle Creek; there were 270, 355, 525, and 575, respectively, for the years 1880, 1890, 1900, and 1910; in that last year, there were 690 blacks residing in Calhoun County. In Allegan and Van Buren Counties, the black population increased from 33 and 99 in 1870 to 247 and 701, respectively, in 1904. In 1910 the count was 241 and 535, respectively, for those two counties. That same year Cass County had 1,444 blacks.[12]

Industrialization in the early 1900s enticed many blacks to pack up and move to Michigan. The foundries, for example, hired recruiters to canvass the economically depressed cotton-producing southern states for laborers. Malleable Iron Company in Albion paid the passage fares for between fifty and seventy-five men from Pensacola, Florida, with the condition that they work in the foundry. Similarly, "man catchers" employed by the sheet metal foundries in Muskegon County did the same thing around Yazoo County, Mississippi and Camden and Magnolia, Arkansas. During that same time period, Muskegon County's population grew accordingly: in 1865 there were 28; in 1870, 40; in 1880, 85; in 1890, 105; in 1900, 53; in 1910, 79; in 1920, 254; in 1930, 1,376; and in 1940, 1,781. They lived mostly near the eastern end of downtown Muskegon, in the Pine Street and Walnut Avenue area.

Interviews with some of the descendants of Michigan's early settlers are very revealing, whether they lived in Kalamazoo, Port Huron, Benton Harbor, Detroit, or Flint. An interview with Mrs. Ruth Owens Buckner revealed that her grandfather, Martin Owens, was an escaped slave from the South. He was placed in a crate and loaded on a boat bound for Ohio. He worked for a while in Ann Arbor, Michigan, before deciding that he would be safer further north in Canada. He later left Canada and arrived in Flint in 1877. Mrs. Buckner's grandmother, Minerva Wright Harris, was a charter member of Quinn Chapel African Methodist Episcopal Church (c. 1875) and her husband, Albert Harris, is said to be one of the first black entrepreneurs in Flint. They had eight children, one of whom was Mrs. Buckner's mother, Alberta Harris.

As a point of interest, Helen Hill Graves was the first black child born in Genesee County, in a house downtown on Saginaw Street. Others, such as the Wrights, the Storums, the Hills, and the Graves, were farmers and laborers, but there were also barbers and at least one fish dealer in the late 1800s.

They came—free blacks, freed blacks, and escaped slaves alike—but did they make any contributions to Michigan? David Katzman offers an insightful answer to this query:

> There was no time in Michigan's past when it was a society of only whites. From the earliest beginnings blacks accompanied the French Jesuits, fur trappers and habitants into the wilderness that later became the present state of Michigan. In the great period of state building, the years between the opening of the Erie Canal in 1825 and the decade of the Civil War in 1860, Michigan Negroes were an indispensable part of the fabric of society.
>
> Although disfranchised until after the Civil War, they nonetheless contributed heavily to the benevolent and reform movements of their day. Michigan's blacks not only raised their voices for abolition and enfranchisement, but also for temperance, women's suffrage, free education and religious revival. Simply as people, also as soldiers, but especially as oral and political reformers, they left their mark in helping to build Michigan.[13]

The Search For "Good Money" Era: 1890s to Present Urbanization

Michigan's black population increased dramatically as a result of the major exodus from the South during and after World War I and World War II. The South's low wages, floods, boll weevil infestations, and the North's industrial expansion and higher wages were among the pushes and pulls, respectively, responsible for thousands of blacks to migrate to Michigan. Detroit, Flint, Hamtramck, Saginaw, Pontiac, River Rouge, Jackson, Lansing, Inkster, Romulus, Ecorse, Mt. Clemens, New Haven, Port Huron, Grand Rapids, Muskegon Heights, Jackson, and Albion were among the main magnet cities. None, of course, was as magnetic as Detroit, which never relinquished its lead in attracting blacks into the state. Its black population in 1994 had nearly a seventy-five percent share of that city's total population of 992,038 people.

Detroit witnessed incredible growth. In 1860, there were 1,403 blacks; in 1870, 2,235; in 1880, 2,821; in 1890, 3,431; in 1900, 4,111; in 1910, 5,741, and in 1920 there were 40,838 black residents.[14] Many blacks were lured to Detroit (also Flint, Pontiac, and other cities) because of job opportunities in the auto industry and especially Henry Ford's offer of five dollars for a day's work. Employment for blacks in the motor industry usually meant working on jobs that were monotonous, dull, backbreaking, dangerous, and injurious to one's health. Not all blacks, of course, came to Detroit to work in the factories as laborers; some were professionals. For example, in 1910, there were 10 clergy, 11 lawyers, 58 musicians, and six physicians. By 1920, there were 82 clergymen, 24 dentists, 32 lawyers, 106 musicians and 28 physicians. Naturally, due to the Jim Crow syndrome, their clientele was black.[15] Some of the frustrations experienced by many black workers in the auto industry from 1920 to 1990 is expressed in a song written and recorded by Joe L. Carter. His words, while extolling work, cry out:

> Please, Mr. Foreman, slow down your assembly line.
> Please, Mr. Foreman, slow down your assembly line.
> No, I don't mind workin', but I do mind dyin'.
> Workin' twelve hours a day,
> Seven long days a week,
> I lie down and try to rest, but Lord knows I'm too tired to sleep.
> Please, Mr. Foreman, slow down your assembly line.
> I said, Lord, why don't you slow down that assembly line?
> No, I don't mind workin', but I do mind dyin'.'[16]

As already noted, the large influx of black migrants contributed enormously to the urban and industrial growth of Michigan's cities. Two General Motors companies, Buick and Chevrolet, were among those heavily involved in the recruitment of blacks to Flint. Old-timers tell interesting stories about how the company built houses for its white workers but largely ignored the housing needs of black workers. Thus, as the Poles, Germans, Lithuanians, and other European immigrants

Figure 4. Norm "Tige" Davis uses his rig to advertise a hairdressing business: Starting a small business requires a lot of work, but little capital; thus, it is a common way for an immigrant or individual without assets to get a financial base to start life. (From the Benjamin C. Wilson Collection. Black Americana Studies Department. Western Michigan University).

moved out of the St. John area (northeast side of the city), blacks moved in and took advantage of the available housing. When this section of the city became a blighted area, it was bought out by Buick for expansion purposes. As a result, many blacks moved into the Evergreen Valley community, which at the time was a white community in transition. Evergreen Valley is now a predominantly black community. The population of Flint in 1990 was 140,761; of that number, there were 67, 485 blacks (48 percent), 69,788 whites (49.6 percent), and 3,488 others (2.4 percent).

Today blacks live in virtually all of the prestigious communities in and around Flint, but there are still problem areas. Flint's northside is one such area. Auto plant closings added enormously to the unemployment rate in this community, already hard hit by crime, drug trafficking, gang problems, high dropout rates, and other social ills.

The new and unprecedented expansion of Michigan's urban areas, however, was problematic for many blacks who had to adjust, for the first time, to city life. For many, life in the city meant a change in their

Figure 5. Early members of the Roberts family in Kalamazoo. (From the Benjamin C. Wilson Collection. Black Americana Studies Department. Western Michigan University).

Figure 6. Willis Roberts, the "iceman," is a descendant of Enoch Harris, who was a freeman from Ohio. He also is a relative of Duane Roberts, a prominent individual in Michigan (From the Benjamin C. Wilson Collection. Black Americana Studies Department. Western Michigan University).

attitudes, ideas, values, and old habits. The habit of eating on the front
porch and throwing food scraps in the yard (delights for chickens and
other farm animals) was an acceptable practice "down home," but
frowned upon in the city. Hence, many of the black newcomers were
chided into eliminating their "countrified ways" (e.g., loud or boister-
ous behavior or the wearing of bright-colored "monkey" clothes).
Consequently, for many, city life was part of an alien society.

The city was a place where black people were forced to live in over-
crowded, segregated neighborhoods, attend segregated schools and
churches, and be excluded from hotels and restaurants and other public places. In short, they were forced into black communities (ghettos)
in the oldest and the most dilapidated sections that were located close
to the central areas of the city.[17] In some cities, such sections were well
established during the antebellum years.

Although seriously challenged by city life, it should be noted that the
black newcomers brought with them a legacy that, combined with that
of the black pioneers, helped enormously in their struggle against many
obstacles. Part of this legacy was their faith and trust in their community churches, their church auxiliaries, their popular culture (music,
special cuisine, etc.), their social and civic organizations, their devotion
to hard work, their intellectual leaders, and their ability to cultivate
"good morals, establish moral reforms, habits of industry, thrift, education and temperance."[18] According to Richard W. Thomas:

> In 1915, when Michigan blacks published the Michigan Manual of
> Freemen's Progress, Detroit blacks, figured prominently in their record of
> black progress. . . . Evidently blacks in Michigan felt confident enough to
> celebrate their progress. In the last few decades, they had proven to them-
> selves and others that they could "achieve wonders on their own." This
> was a new class of blacks, proud of their accomplishments as black peo-
> ple. They believed in building from strength rather than lamenting their
> weaknesses, and they embodied the best of the black self-help tradition
> of the period.[19]

A belief that they could "achieve wonders on their own" has enabled
Michigan's black sons and daughters to make their presence felt in

Figure 7. The Second Baptist Church and Congregation in Kalamazoo, Michigan (From the Benjamin C. Wilson Collection. Black Americana Studies Department. Western Michigan University).

business, politics, government, manufacturing, literature, music (especially jazz, spirituals, blues, and gospel), art, dance, drama, science, education, medicine, sports, folk culture, and valorous service in all the nation's wars. From everyday folk to the most notable figures in public and private life, blacks have made immeasurable contributions to Michigan's heritage. In this same context, David Katzman asserts the following:

> Whether they were tilling the soil in Southwestern Michigan, or mining ore in the Upper Peninsula, or cutting lumber in the Saginaw Bay region, or barbering in any of the hundred small agricultural villages scattered across the state, rural Negroes left their mark in the building of Michigan.[20]

Current Issues Facing the Black Community

Unemployment

While thrift, industry, and hard work helped elevate many blacks into a middle-class or upper-class status, more than fifty percent of the black

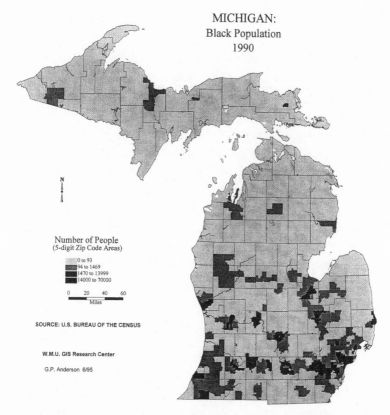

MICHIGAN:
Black Population
1990

Number of People
(5-digit Zip Code Areas)

0 to 93
94 to 1469
1470 to 13999
14000 to 70000

0   20   40   60
Miles

SOURCE: U.S. BUREAU OF THE CENSUS

W.M.U. GIS Research Center

G.P. Anderson 6/95

Figure 8. Distribution of Michigan's Population Claiming African American Identity (1990).

citizens in Michigan are on the lower rung of the status ladder. Consequently, and unarguably, tens of thousands of the state's black citizens—rural and urban alike—face staggering problems on a daily basis, and "despite the momentous changes taking place in other arenas during the 1980s, the movement to gain economic equality for blacks stalled."[21] As the decade of the 1990s comes to a close, blacks continue to find themselves greatly over-represented in low-paying jobs while vastly underrepresented in such professions as engineering, medicine, architecture, law, dentistry, geology, and others.

The unemployment situation in Detroit today has not changed dramatically from that of a decade ago. At that time the figures showed an average unemployment rate, from 1981 to 1985, for black men and women to be thirty and twenty-nine percent. For whites during the same five-year period, the rates were 9.7 percent for men and 10.2 percent for women. For the state of Michigan, blacks experienced a 28.7 percent unemployment rate, while whites had a 10.6 rate of unemployment. These figures demonstrate the continuation of a pattern of disparity and inequity which underlies much of the poverty for blacks in Michigan.[22] Unfortunately, this pattern continues to exist even when Michigan's economy is vibrant and strong, and as the U.S. society continues to make significant gains on many fronts in group relations.

The unemployment picture for the black youth in the state has been very bleak for more than a decade. In some black neighborhoods the jobless rate for young people exceeds the 40 percent mark, and these are the same neighborhoods where the enormous drug trafficking and crime problems are typically found. Thus, the future for many black youths, especially males, is not an optimistic one at this time.

Housing

While there continues to be strong resistance to integrated neighborhoods—witness patterns of white flight to the suburbs in virtually every city in Michigan—blacks have acquired wealth and status to live outside the economically depressed areas. For example, in the metropolitan area of Detroit, blacks reside in Bloomfield Hills, West Bloomfield, even a few in Birmingham and Grosse Point. In Detroit proper, there are black/white mixed areas composed mainly of professional people: Rosedale Park and New Center are such areas. They are substantial neighborhoods and relatively crime-free. Those blacks who do not have housing worries are indeed fortunate because, according to John O. Calmore:

> The "disadvantageous distinction" of being black in America probably presents its most diverse, complex, and intractable problems in our attempts to secure viable property rights and housing opportunities. Problems associated with where we live, under what conditions, and why, have plagued Black America since slavery. Indeed, the continual push for equal treatment and real housing opportunities has been Black America's

Sisyphean Rock. While this rock has grown appreciably lighter for some, its general tendency nonetheless is to persist in rolling back to the bottom of our hill. And this tendency impacts most severely on the 36% of poor black Americans.[23]

Michigan, like the rest of the country, has yet to solve the dilemma of housing discrimination. The 1968 Civil Rights Act has been ineffectual in dealing with the housing problems for blacks and other minorities. Patterns of exploitation and discrimination in housing continue to persist despite legislative efforts to the contrary. On many occasions, writers have wondered what happened to the black residents who once resided where the Silverdome is now located, or those who lived on or near Logan Street/Martin Luther King Boulevard in Lansing. Is urban renewal simply a euphemism for black/minority removal?

Family

The number of black families headed by single females, who have never been married, increased from 12 percent in 1960 to 55 percent in 1993. During this time, the number of black families that lived in poverty more than tripled in some urban areas. It is estimated that at least half of all black families with children are headed by women, many of whom are among the poorest of the poor in Michigan. On the one hand, however, many of these single females are to be commended for doing a remarkable job of rearing their children under very trying circumstances. On the other hand, a growing concern exists over teenage pregnancies—"babies having babies." This concern extends to an increasing number of babies born to mothers on "crack" cocaine, infected with the AIDS virus, or too immature or impoverished to give their children a fighting chance for a decent life. Black male teenagers, heavily involved in this deplorable situation, are not ignored as part of this problem. Many babies have teenaged fathers who are dependent on their own parents for support, who therefore cannot provide for their children's welfare, and who may be simply uninterested in their offspring because the relationship with the mothers was thought to be nothing more than a frivolous sexual encounter.[24]

Education

Education, long viewed as one of the primary conduits out of poverty and the black ghetto, no longer serves that function for scores of black children. Ghetto schools are in a state of crisis; children are dropping out at an alarming rate and too many of those who do manage to graduate are unable to read, write, and compute at a level necessary to perform well in a high-tech society. At the collegiate level, black undergraduate enrollment has been rebounding from a decline that started over a decade ago in 1986.[25] An increase, for example, shows up in recent figures at the University of Michigan (Ann Arbor), which had a black enrollment of 8.1 percent, and Wayne State University, which had a twenty-four percent black enrollment on its campus.[26] In 1996, 60,544 blacks students enrolled in Michigan's colleges. The black male enrollment, however, remained low, especially when compared to their incarceration rate: more black males are in prisons than in college.

Health

Clifford L Broman's assessment of the health status of blacks in Michigan is as pertinent today as it was in 1987. At that time, he observed that:

> Although it is true that the health status of Americans is generally improving, the disparity in health status between black and white Americans persists . . . the black infant mortality rate was approximately twice that of whites, and death rates for all other major causes of death—heart disease, cancer, cerebrovascular disease, homicide, accidents, and diabetes—exceeded the rate for whites. . . . The causes for this disparity in health status are varied, but the evidence suggests strongly that socioeconomic factors play an important role.[27]

The general health status of blacks has not kept pace with that of whites in the state. For example, in Kalamazoo County, the neonatal death rate is "nearly three times as high among black infants than white infants," and the postneonatal death rate for black infants is double that of white infants.[28] In recent years, the disproportionate incidence of AIDS in the black community has contributed dramatically to an

already unsatisfactory health picture. It is anticipated that AIDS, especially since there is no cure for this dreaded disease, will continue to
spread among "high risk" groups, such as drug users who share needles
and those who are bisexual in their sexual orientations. There is an
anticipated tenfold increase in AIDS among the heterosexual black
population in Michigan over the next several years.[29] Because of these
conditions, and other factors, it is doubtful that a major improvement
in the health status of blacks will be made in the near future. Also, the
failure of President Clinton's administration to reform the country's
health care system does not bode well for those residing in the more
fragile communities.

The Black Community: Bright or Bleak Future?

Self-help initiatives notwithstanding, the enormity of some problems
found in the black community suggests that adequate solutions are
most unlikely to be found any time soon. In many black communities
the resources for dealing with these problems are too meager and the
local leadership is either woefully inadequate or virtually nonexistent.
This is especially true for those who live in abject poverty, a poverty
characterized by welfare dependency, high dropout and illiteracy rates,
high unemployment, domestic violence, inadequate school systems,
high crime and delinquency rates, high infant mortality rates, drug
abuse and drug trafficking, unmet health needs, a growing AIDS men-
ace, and homelessness. These are neighborhoods where black citizens
are afraid to walk the streets at night and are constantly concerned
about their property and personal welfare.

Social problems in economically depressed black communities are
ominous and foreboding, which means that effective ameliorative strategies are urgently needed. In this connection, there are many positive
signs in cities across the state of Michigan, with Detroit being one of the
major leaders in making significant progress on numerous fronts. Paula
Farmer, in an excellent article on the renaissance of Detroit, notes that:

> The dependency index is another indicator of a city's well-being. This
> index reveals the percentage of the employed population that is on

welfare and the total percentage of unemployment in the city. And that ratio is down. In fact, from 1993 to 1997, the unemployment rate has dropped by half, going from 13.6% to 7.8%. The average household income for Detroit has grown by 3%, from $34,710 in 1995 to $35,748 in 1996. The city ranks eleventh in income for the nation.[30]

Under Mayor Dennis Archer's leadership, the city of Detroit has rapidly regained some of its lost prestige as a world-class city. General Motors, Ford, and Chrysler (the city's Big Three automotive companies) have played a major role in contributing to the employment and tax base of the city. The employment outlook is further enhanced with the building of two new sport stadiums, three gambling casinos, and other cultural and entertainment centers and hotels in the downtown area. These and other economic developments are arguably the type of initiatives that will have a profound and lasting impact on African Americans who make up seventy-six percent of that city's population. In brief, the current outlook is much brighter for many African Americans than a decade ago. This is also true for many other African Americans who live elsewhere in Michigan. However, there are still those black Americans who get little or no relief from living a life in abject poverty; and there appears to be no comprehensive set of strategies to move them out of that existence.

A viable blueprint has yet to be designed because researchers, scholars, political leaders, and everyday citizens continue to be at odds, often bitterly so, over the nature of black problems and their causes and solutions. Among the different voices, there are those who think the problems of blacks in Michigan will be solved by: (1) little or no government intervention; (2) a radical shift toward a socialist system; (3) the elimination of joblessness, i.e., full employment; (4) more effective domestic programs; (5) the mobilization of strengths through more black self-help programs; (6) a more Afrocentric approach; and the list goes on.

Conservatives and neoconservatives, both blacks and whites, argue that the government has no viable role in the amelioration of social problems of black people, or anyone else for that matter. The government should have a hands-off policy that lets each individual pursue his or her own self-interest in his or her own way within a free enterprise system.[31] The neoconservative strategy of the last several years, then, has emphasized self-help, individual freedom, and personal responsibility as the fundamental means for anyone—black or white—to achieve equality in the American context. Neo-marxists, on the other hand, continue to be extremely critical of U.S. capitalism as a system capable of distributing wealth and justice in an equitable and fair manner. They envision a society free of "all forms of colonial ripoff," and, in time, the regeneration of self-determining black communities.[32]

Those advocating an Afrocentric perspective tend to view it as essential to the restoration of the appropriate and necessary sociocultural values of "Mother Africa," an orientation calling for the creation of an African-based cultural community of different varieties. Thus, African Americans, not unlike the Dutch, Greeks, Jews, Poles, Germans, Italians, and other groups in this country, will come to see themselves in a new light, as a contributing people with value and worth.

Still others think that black people must be responsible for their own salvation and liberation. They see the problem as one of proper management of the resources and strengths that black people have in their own communities. Taking advantage of state and federal social programs and initiatives in the process is not seen as inconsistent with their liberation. It is very consistent because other groups, especially the wealthy and powerful, have used the government in advancing their own self-interests; therefore, blacks should not be criticized for doing the same thing.

It is evident, then, that the problems in the black community will neither be approached by a single voice nor a single, unified group. In another context, the senior author wrote:

> We would argue, however, that because of the magnitude and complexity of the race problems perhaps . . . a multifaceted approach may disrupt the equilibrium of a racist system sufficiently to bring about a new order—without exploitation, oppression, and racism—for all of the peoples regardless of race, creed, nationality, religion or color.[33]

As the current debates rage on, however, the poor will struggle onward in silence, accepting and embracing each moment of relief as a precious gift because they know tomorrow—or the next minute—will come and they must face again the ugly realities of poverty and its attendant problems. The debate also will continue while thousands of African Americans struggle desperately to solidify their newly acquired middle-class status in an fiercely competitive world. At the same time, the BUPPIES (black upwardly mobile) and "old-money folk" will drive their expensive cars, call the office on their cellular phones, discuss major transactions over lunch at their fashionable restaurants and, being well-fed, will extol the virtues of "living well" in Michigan. They have money, expensive jewels, fancy cars, tailored clothes, fine homes, and a "somebody" status. Like their less fortunate black brothers and sisters, however, they cannot altogether escape racism in Michigan and the larger society. There are some critics who feel that too many African Americans who have "made it" have forgotten their roots; that, although sympathetic, their sense of peoplehood is not deep and com-pelling enough for them to lend their talents, skills, and knowledge in the eradication of the numerous social ills that continue to plague the poorer black communities in Michigan's urban and rural areas.

As the society enters the next millennium, we can only hope that from among the competing ideologies and strategies, there will emerge a viable plan or blueprint to help those who are less fortunate. Using the past as an indicator, we feel safe in concluding that African Americans in Michigan will draw hope and strength from the knowl-edge that they are part of a legacy that has survived tremendous chal-lenges in the past. Moreover, though their problems are difficult and complex, they will persist in their struggle for a fuller and richer life and, in the process, continue to contribute significantly to Michigan's heritage.

Ethnicity in Identity Politics in the Schooling Experiences of African American High School Students

Linwood H. Cousins

Introduction

Reaching beyond the borders of Michigan, this article discusses schooling or education and ethnic identity politics, relevant to the contemporary situation of African Americans in this state. This discussion focuses on the predominantly black city of Newark, New Jersey, where African Americans have historical and contemporary problems that are parallel, though with subtle and important differences, to those of African Americans in Michigan cities such as Detroit, Flint, and Saginaw. Newark and Detroit, among other urban industrial cities, were major sites of black migration from the South. Even the foundations and proliferation of the Nation of Islam link Detroit and Newark through W. D. Farad or Master Farad Muhammad, the leader of the Black Muslim Movement in Detroit, who served as the inspiration behind Elijah Muhammad and drew followers from Newark.[1] The social and political thrust of the Nation of Islam is perhaps one end of the continuum of Afrocentrism that permeates Newark and Detroit.

Still, after World War II, Newark and Detroit had the attraction of booming economies coupled with the appearance of less racism than the South. However, over the last thirty years these cities have faced problems associated with the rising and falling tides of local and regional industries, and the relocation of some industries to the outer suburbs which has been accompanied by white flight in general and black middle-class flight in particular. The rise and fall of local and regional economies have destabilized black income and employment rates in these cities, and have traumatized local tax bases by which schools are partially funded. Additional effects shared by these cities have been high rates of single-parent families, teen pregnancy, and school dropout. What's more, both cities have faced the paradox of an increase in black leadership (mayors, city council members, and school board representatives) but a decrease in the economic wealth and prosperity such cities need to remain socially and economically viable.[2]

Where they differ is that Newark and northern New Jersey have a higher population density than Detroit and other Michigan cities. Detroit, for example is comprised of about 138.7 square miles, has had a population hovering around one million people for the last decade and a half, with more than eighty percent of them African American. By contrast, Newark's population has hovered around 300,000 within an area of twenty-three square miles, with African Americans comprising a majority of the population. And while Newark has not had the economic benefits and liabilities associated with Detroit's auto industry, Newark boasts the bane and blessing of being nestled between New York and Philadelphia, ethnically mixed port cities and economic powerhouses.

Another interesting relationship exists between Newark and Detroit. Indeed, several, mostly African American and Hispanic school districts in New Jersey, including Newark, preceded Detroit in facing the takeover of school boards because of failing school systems.[3] More importantly, any close reading of these school conflicts reveals deep-seated racial and ethnic politics and conflict within the ethnic or racial groups involved, and between these groups and the mostly white state governments that aim to seize control of the failing schools.

As such, this article discusses African American ethnicity as an important but elusive feature of life in America because of the omnipresence of race, and to a lesser extent, class. I will attempt to explain the elusiveness of African American ethnicity as both separateness and togetherness or "we-ness and they-ness."[4] I will do this by presenting subjective viewpoints from the life and community of black

The Detroit public schools will be taken over by Mayor Dennis Archer by the opening of the next school year. A state takeover of the Oakland, California public schools is being threatened, and the school governance will change drastically in Prince George's County, MD. Why? Legislators and policymakers are desperately searching for ways to improve learning. And report cards from critics of schools in Michigan, California and Maryland are similar: Dropout rates are too high. Kids aren't learning. Failure rates on standardized tests are excessive. And school boards have been unable, or unwilling, to respond to the problems. But Michigan Senate Majority Leader Dan DeGrow, R-Port Huron, sponsor of the Detroit takeover bill, says school systems like Detroit's need new management: "The Detroit board has a 20-year history of failure. Clearly an overwhelming majority of people, both in the city of Detroit and the state, feel that it was time for a major change."

—*Excerpt from* USA Today; *30 March 1999: "School takeovers: Officials and activists collide."*

high school students to implicate, ultimately, the meaning of African American identity politics for multicultural education.

Despite the dominance of race as an organizing concept in black-white relations in America, ethnicity retains characteristics that are useful to explaining black life here. For African Americans, ethnicity merges with race in its entailment of social formations and interactions—within and outside black mental and spatial communities—aimed at distinguishing who black people are and who they are not. As Jack Glazier notes in the first volume of *Discovering the Peoples of Michigan*, for black people "cultural distinctiveness is reinforced in complex ways through its coincidence with distinctions of skin color, or racial difference, as that phrase is popularly understood."[5] Hence, Fredrik Barth (1969) records that ethnic groups are categories of identification that have "the characteristic of organizing interaction between people;"[6] ethnic categories are "organizational vessels that may be given varying amounts and forms of content in different sociocultural systems;"[7] and ethnic distinctions entail "social processes of exclusion and incorporation."[8]

Abner Cohen similarly notes that "[e]thnicity is essentially a form of interaction between culture groups operating within common social contexts," yet it is a "complex phenomenon that is involved in psychological, historical, economic, and political factors," and can be analyzed in terms of interconnections with political and economic relationships.[9] Comprising to some degree both fluidity and instability, the identity function of ethnicity, according to Cohen, works largely in terms of collective representations that also manifest themselves in individual behavior.[10]

Still, the point of boundary making—the construction of social distinctions among and between groups, shifts in meaning, instability and fluidity, and ambiguities of reference—cannot be overstated as important features operating in the psychic and social-behavioral worlds of African Americans.[11] Calling it a process of "nesting dichotomizations of inclusiveness and exclusiveness" that are historically defined, Ronald Cohen clarifies what is implicit in ethnicity.[12] In his ethnographic exploration of an African American community in Washington, D.C., for example, Ulf Hannerz recorded internal and external categories of identity and other coded distinctions— respectibles and nonrespectibles, lower class and working class—as essential to the world view engulfing black community life as defined both by black-black and black-white relations.[13] One can find similar practices of distinction in the lives of other ethnic groups in the context of schooling that also focus on internal and external ethnic and class relations.[14]

In sum, many black youth often carry into school settings precariousness, ambivalence, and even radicalism regarding identity that many scholars have discussed mostly in racial and class terms.[15] John Ogbu and Signithia Fordham have captured adolescent identity politics in this respect in their presentation of black students "acting white,"[16] and the experience of "racelessness."[17] But, "acting white" and "racelessness," as parts of identity formations, are more than race concerns because for blacks in America race extends into realms of existence that include the theoretical and conceptual domain of ethnicity—what Glazier in this volume calls conscious "belongingness," defined by culture, language, and history.[18]

Thus, examining what black students believe and practice regarding schooling, education, religion, and community life in general reflects their sense of "belongingness" and the practice of "inclusiveness" in terms of a shared history and common life chances. Examining the students' circumstance in such a context shines a necessary light on the racial and ethnic identity politics that help define the structure and function of ethnicity in America. Below are excerpts taken from my study of Community High (pseudonym) and urban black high school students in Newark, New Jersey. Although the excerpts present the experiences of one school, the experiences are nonetheless representative of many other schools, including high schools in Michigan.[19] Given the economic, social, and political parallels between Newark and Detroit presented earlier, it is no wonder that the schools in these predominately black cities have struggled.[20]

Perceptions of Schooling and Education

What is most striking about the perceptions and practices of black high school students is the incongruity between their desire for an education and their successful participation in the schooling process. When asked to share their beliefs and plans for school success for the remainder of the school year, Bobby, a senior in high school, stated: "I plan to keep up with my work by reading more, studying more, and paying attention in class so I will have a better understanding of the things that I am learning. I plan to set aside at least two hours for my study." Cheryl, a senior who immigrated to America from Guyana, said: "In relation to my studies, I would like to spend much more time studying every night. Before [,] doing my homework was what I considered as studying. Now I realize that it takes a lot more, especially with my aspiration to be a scholar student."

Finally, Mack, a senior who is very conscious of race and ethnicity, said that

1993 is the year in which I [will] explode into something we know as society. The surrounding for me will be a new college scene, as I [will] be challenged to function at a higher level. I stood in 1992 with my arms stretched

Figure 1. View of Community High.

out for this challenge and now that it's on the tip of my fingers, I accept
this challenge totally. I desire this challenge because it will enable me to
better myself, give me all [the] opportunities to prove to this world that I
am a man. I understand that a college education is the road to success
and I feel if that's what it takes, that's what they will get from me and after
that, the [white] "man" will never see me face to face again. In the year
1993, the man has arrived.

Each of the students quoted above graduated in the upper ranks of
their class in 1993, but none of them achieved the academic success of
which they were capable. Their participation in schooling was attenu-
ated by a social environment, extending from their community, in
which being too cooperative, too active, or studying too hard and doing
too much homework suggested too much trust in a white or mainstream educational system that repeatedly fails and misleads black
people based on the lived experiences these students saw in their families, in their neighborhoods, and among community members.
The academic performance ceiling that black students placed over
themselves represents a combination of adolescent identity formation

intermingled with the past, and the contemporary history of race relations in their segregated community—all of which provide the material from which adolescents draw to imagine their futures and plan the very next steps in their lives. Other examples follow.

Representing another angle on the students' interpretation of classroom activities and curriculum is a classroom discussion of Ralph Waldo Emerson's essay "Self Reliance." Two juniors, Tim and Ahmad, aspire to go to college for careers in engineering and teaching, respectively, and responded as follows to the teacher's question about the meaning of the essay to them: "You can't rely on anybody. You can't rely on your own people, you can't rely on your mother." All the students in the class were struck by their responses, not wanting what they said to be an accurate representation of reality but all the while knowing it was true.

In another English class in which students were discussing Emerson, Ali, also a junior, offered the following comment when asked by the teacher to give his interpretation of the vocabulary words "conspire" and "conformity." He simply said they mean "there is a pull to be like white people." Seniors in a group discussion were responding to the question "What's important in life?" The boys said "money, which you get the best way you can, selling drugs or whatever." The girls said "education and happiness" are the important things in life. The boys again responded: "It all comes back to money. If there wasn't no money there would be no education, no school, no happiness."

As a final excerpt in this section on perceptions of education and schooling, I present the case of Randall, followed by a few comments from parents. Randall was a senior at the top of the class in academics and sports, but he was one of the most alienated students in the school. The teachers generally told me they considered Randall an enigma, an aloof person. Following are comments Randall made in a conversation we had about his perception of schooling. He began by challenging his own high status and recognition among his peers:

> Why should I be acknowledged above my peers? A lot of other people deserve recognition too. But we ignore them. When Carl Lewis won the 100 meter dash he was the only one on the cover of *Sports Illustrated*.

Figures 2 and 3. Scenes inside Community High.

What about those guys who ran in the race with him. They are some of the fastest humans in the world like Lewis. That is what they want me to do at this school and I refuse. Then they try to make me [be a leader]. They can't make me! How does that sound?

During my participation in PTA meetings and other parent-teacher activities, I gained a sense of how the parents faced very real dilemmas because of the historical mistrust between white-controlled institutions such as schools and the black communities they serve even though schools are necessary for black students' economic and career success. During one of these meetings in which we were talking about the limited academic success of our black students, I said, "Students often don't come to class with books and paper, and they come late [or not at all]. The teachers I observe are patient and very supportive with their students, but over the last seven months I have not seen the students improve." Despite being African American, the parents did not deem my comments acceptable in terms of their and their communities' realities. Several parents immediately gave examples of teachers who have been inappropriate, and examples of how the children are doing the best that they can given the circumstances in their community. Finally one parent said the following:

> We need an active demonstration demanding the things we need. They [white people] say we don't care about our children. We do care about our children. Our kids need proper guidance. You don't go to no high school and can't [learn or come out not being able to] read? My boys go be som'n! Time for us to do for our own kids. They [white people and people in the suburbs] always talk about black people want'n something from them. These kids can do, they are very resourceful.

Many parents responded "amen, amen" to these remarks.

In sum, the students and parents here are constantly expressing their identity struggles through their practices in school and their interpretation of the school's curriculum and social processes, all in the context of lived experience in their community. Certainly the students make interpretations that limit their performance and motivation, and certainly the parents seem to make excuses for the students' limitations. Yet the students and parents are operating within the bounds of their everyday experiences as influenced by both the past and present, whether real or imagined. To discount these processes is to diminish their reality and influence, and miss the opportunity to understand identity formation—the seeds of culture and ethnicity—in process.

Perceptions in the Realm of Religion

Church life and religion have held central roles in the life and identity of black communities. Originating as bulwarks against the tides of cruelty during slavery and afterwards, black churches continually evolved as radical institutions playing a major role in the politics of race and political and economic equality in American society.[21] Such an interpretation fits well with an important original black interpretation of religion as a "tangible symbol of distinction."[22] I contend here that an examination of the interpretation of students' religious perceptions offers additional insight into ethnic and racial identity formation, and provides linkages to understanding black students' overall world view.

Increasingly black adolescents are attracted to radical forms of religious practice such as the Nation of Islam, even though they continue to participate more often in conventional black church experiences represented by Baptists and others. The philosophy of the Nation of Islam offers black students an opportunity to affirm their ethnic identity in history—with its particular focus on African tradition and origins—while participating in current activities and rhetoric that allow them to vent their feelings of alienation and mistreatment by white America. The Nation couples such an identity process with the building of self-control, discipline, and self-esteem. Below I present excerpts from students who embrace these concepts. Bobby, a senior, told me a little about his religious beliefs:

> Like when I was little, I 'um kinda almost got away from religion totally. 'Cause I had this Bible, it was a picture Bible. And all the pictures in the Bible, all you saw was white people, you know. And my mother, I asked my mother why. She told me that there were black people in the Bible, but you know, I still didn't believe her. I thought white people were the only people that went to heaven. White people were the only people that God wanted, and stuff like that.

Bobby's statement is representative of many of the high school students I knew. His dialogues in his classes attested to his radical and passionate sense of blackness or black identity that is associated with ethnicity, flowing from his interpretation of self in the context of white-black relations.

Carl, another senior, talked to me about wanting to get into "the Muslim religion." He was not doing well in school, and he told me that school is irrelevant to the things he wants to do with his life. Carl plans to go to trade school after he graduates. My friends and I used to say the same things about school when we attended junior high and high school. It was our, and I believe Carl's, crude way of saying we were bored and disconnected from the process of schooling as we knew it, and disconnected from the academic track that would stream us into college. We, like Carl, knew very little about college during high school. On the other hand, the world of pragmatic trades—carpentry, plumbing, auto mechanics, and brick-masonry in our black working class community—were things we came to see as very practical and realistic. Such an environment and attitude permeated our community life, as it had Carl's.

Still, Carl wanted to get into the "Muslim religion." Why? First he said it was because his father was involved, and he said:

> 'Cause a lot of Muslims (Nation of Islam in particular), they talk deep [insightful about the origins of the oppression of black people and the rituals of religious sanctity, for example]. They talk real deep. They deep in their religion. I like that. And plus, what they say about the white man and stuff like that. Like what Malcolm X said.

For many black students, religion is a realm of their community experience that intersects with other aspects of their identity formation. Although many adolescents are ambivalent and ambiguous about their religious identity during this stage of their development, I believe nonetheless that such incipient practices implicate significant elements of cultural schemas in identity formation that should not be radically separated from explorations of the type undertaken here and elsewhere in Discovering the Peoples of Michigan.

Intersections between Community and School

The fluidity of black identity across the boundaries of school, community, and family life confronts an individualistic and overly self-reliant approach to life propagated in current attitudes and social policies of dominant political platforms in America. In other words, who people are is more than a function of one sphere of their lives. Thus, to understand them one must observe or explore a people's multidimensionality.

During the latter half of the school year in Newark in 1993, the school district faced imminent takeover by state authorities due to alleged academic and fiscal mismanagement. Many states, including Michigan, California, and Maryland, have considered or enforced similar action in predominantly black and or Hispanic schools in urban areas. Rather than perceive the takeover as action on the part of a faceless state bureaucracy, many black teachers, students, parents, and politicians in Newark defined the proposed takeover as issues of racial and ethnic competence, emancipation, and oppression (see the sidebar for examples of similar issues in Detroit's school takeover). One teacher who agreed that the schools needed to do better in educating students still felt that the proposed takeover meant more:

> The takeover action is a perpetuation of the myth that black children can't learn and aren't learning. It is a case of the great white fathers coming to the aid of black people again. It might be less the case if they were going to infuse more money into the system. It is a ruse. They will come in, show us what to do, and [literally] leave before dark [because they fear for their safety in black communities].

In the next excerpt one will again see the fluidity of maneuvers in identity formations and alliances in discourses implying social, racial, ethnic, and political boundaries drawn in terms of the proposed state takeover action. At a city school board meeting I attended I recorded the following dialogue regarding the takeover action. The president of the city's school board, a black man, warned the state that an attempt to take over the schools would unleash a "war" in which the city and the school board would "take no prisoners." He went on to suggest that anybody who got in the way would be considered an enemy, including black politicians and leaders. Another black school board member said that the takeover would be doomed to failure because these "outsiders" [whites and others] would try to impose a "plantation mentality" on the school system by ignoring [black] local residents and officials.

Such discourse builds alliances within groups as much as it creates divisions between groups. Inciting identity through race and ethnic community affiliation and loyalty is an old maneuver but one that continues to play well today. This kind of maneuvering is particularly effective in cities and schools that are increasingly homogenized in terms of race and socio-economic status. Not being immune to the above discourses that are enacted publicly, black and white students are forced to choose sides before they even understand the issues. Hence, in many instances students take on identity by default. Students identify with whichever side of the racial and ethnic fence they happen to be living on during the time adults are working out the politics of inequality and power over resources such as education in their respective communities.

In these situations, black students vividly transmit many of the ideals of identity portrayed and prized in their communities and society at large. I will present aspects of such identity as transmitted in the aesthetic sphere of school life. These examples represent the improvisational practices of students as they expressed their racial and ethnic identities through reshaping and reinterpreting mainstream fashion and taste, as a jazz musician or a black gospel singer would improvise a song like "Amazing Grace." Identity as played out in these discourses represents another intersection between school, family, and community life.

I present here excerpts of my observations from "Colors of The Spirit: A Fashion Pageant," a fashion show conducted by seniors at the high school. The pageant was held in the school auditorium on a Friday evening at 7:00 P.M. The event was largely the domain of young women in terms of participation and planning. Students who participated in the pageant were diligent in their preparation, making certain they were "just right" so that they could "have it going on" as they strolled across the stage. If they didn't have things just right, they knew they would be "dissed" (in other words, dismissed, ridiculed, and embarrassed). The main event began with formal wear fashion followed by

Figure 4. Students Mixing Attitudes and Attire at the Senior Prom.

casual wear, a talent phase in which students sang or danced, and a question and answer session. Such a format is modeled after the Miss America or Miss Black America Pageant. The music for the school's pageant, however, was hip hop, rap, and rhythm and blues, (including artists such as TLC, LeVert, and En Vogue). Yet the styles of dress in the formal wear segment were mostly evening gowns and tuxedos like the ones seen in the *Ebony Fashion Fair*, mainstream fashion magazines, and displayed in windows of expensive department stores.

Some of the modeled casual clothes were also mainstream in appearance and somewhat plain and demure: pinstriped rugby shirts and white shorts, blue sweatsuits, and so forth. Other students modeled the oversized and brightly colored jeans and shirts that are associated with hip hop and rap subcultural styles. Singing and dancing styles were from the genre of rhythm and blues, as well as hip hop and rap styles seen on "Yo! MTV Raps," BET (Black Entertainment Television), music videos, and the like.

The essence of the matter is the students' interaction with and reinterpretation of mainstream styles of dress and attitudes, which in the process of modeling demonstrated styles of dress and ways of acting preferred by adolescents and young adults in the black world in which these students lived. Specifically, the audience and I were most moved by the students' styles of walking—ways of moving their faces, mouths, arms, hands and eyes—and their ways of dancing, condensed and submerged into a black social pose familiar to many black people. These students merged their attitudes—their persona—with the attire they adorned, reshaping the attire and redefining it in accordance with historically continuous aesthetic values and standards sanctioned among their peers and community members.

The boys presented what I call a "hip hop" strut with a stern, tough, bad boy gaze on their faces. Such styles are popular among young black men and adolescents. In contrast, being "bad" (or outstanding) and "having it going on" for the girls translated into displays of flair and grace in their bodily movements, combined with clothing that was extravagant, and faces and bodies that were stunningly beautiful. The act of modeling by these young women transcended their age and economic status, contradicting the assumptions of style and taste assumed to lie embedded in groups below the middle class in America.

In short, I believe the above snapshots of black life reflect what anthropologists Signithia Fordham and John Ogbu[23] have described as a cultural-ecological process of fusion between black communities, schooling, and the family. In their studies of black schooling, Fordham and Ogbu note that some communities acquire their distinctiveness or separateness, as well as fusion or fluidity between internal institutions, as a result of forced segregation. Fordham and Ogbu further posit that attitudes in black communities are formed in opposition to the mistreatment of blacks by whites in economic, social, and political spheres of lived experience. While I believe that there is some merit to Fordham's and Ogbu's propositions, I further believe that black people's coalescence around things black is an act of arranging one's life in accord with what is emotionally and spatially close, accessible, and familiar—actions common to any ethnic group.

Implications for Multicultural Education

Schools are sites of social/cultural contestation, strain and reproduction, and, consequently, ambivalence and precariousness for involuntary racial/ethnic minorities such as blacks in America. Educational theorist Henry Giroux says that "Schooling is understood as part of the production and legitimization of social forms and subjectivities as they are organized within relations of power and meaning that either enable or limit human capacities for self and social empowerment."[24] Michel Foucault offers a proposition that further illuminates the complex social and cultural fabric of schooling pertaining to identity and ethnicity: "There are three fundamental elements of any experience: a game of truth, relations of power, and forms of relation to oneself and others."[25]

Essentially schooling processes for blacks represent spheres of identity formation that extend beyond the typical development phases children and adolescents experience anyway. Here the game of schooling is more costly because of America's peculiar predicament with race, ethnicity, and black people. Black children and adolescents are carving out their identity within the context of institutional norms and policies—games of truth and relations of power—that *a priori* pathologize or delegitimize and stigmatize the kind of social and behavioral practices and attitudes that represent the way these black citizens express themselves. Yet through a sort of cultural resilience, many of these black citizens resist full assimilation into mainstream forms of life or improvise in such a way as to preserve their own racial and ethnic integrity—the sphere of forms of relations to oneself and others as seen in the students' pageant and their response to Emerson. Often, however, the results of resistance and improvisation are costly in terms of psychological and economic marginalization as demonstrated in students' ambivalence and precariousness expressed in their schooling and religious perceptions and practices.

Thus, successful multicultural schooling begins, conceptually, by examining the footing of power and truth regarding the paradigms of schooling in which there is disproportionate failure for certain populations in society. We need to examine the processes, standards, and curricula of schooling that have been taken as truth. In the process, we do not need to diminish the contributions of theories and processes that were once beneficial, or the forms of power, truth, and authority through which they were sanctioned. Rather, examination and modification accept that there are power imbalances represented in both the knowledge and processes that become incorporated into institutions like schools, and such imbalances need to be adjusted to address shifts in what we know as citizens, educators, and researchers about the effectiveness and ineffectiveness of schooling, and the multiple forms in which inequality and the feigning of truth in schooling manifests itself.

In terms of black citizens, multicultural education must take both the portraits of black life (or the life of any ethnic group) and the interpretations of these portraits as real. People define themselves not just in terms of internal or intragroup relations, but also in terms of external or intergroup relations. The issue here is not so much that the behaviors, attitudes, values, and practices reflected above are limiting for black people. Rather, it is that such actions are historically and culturally continuous for black people in America. These actions represent the very real distinctions that black people make between themselves and whites, or the mainstream, even while coexisting in close proximity to them.

In fact, most African American students possess a deep and abiding concern about education and the quality of life in America. They believe in democracy, freedom, and the inalienable rights of others just as much as any ethnic group. But, because these students participate in a society and educational system constructed within the cultural, social, and political parameters of white mainstream America, black students, as noted earlier, are thrust immediately in the throes of identity development conflict, whether their teachers, educators, or schools are black or white. Outcomes from such a mixture of competing concerns are largely misunderstood inasmuch as incidents of academic failure and low performance, for example, are interpreted largely in narrow cognitive and psychological terms, rather than in terms of the alchemy of culture and strain that represents a more wholesome source of understanding.

Notes

African Americans in Michigan

1. Edna Bonacich, "Racism in Advanced Capitalist Society: Comments on William J. Wilson's *The Truly Disadvantaged*," *Journal of Sociology and Social Welfare* 16, no. 4: 45–46.
2. *Encyclopedia Americana* (New York: Americana Corporation, 1963), 89.
3. David M. Katzman, "Black Slavery in Michigan," *Midcontinent American Studies Journal* 11 (Fall 1970): 60.
4. Ibid., 63.
5. Benjamin C. Wilson, "An Epic of Heroism: The Underground Railroad in Michigan, 1837–1870," *Museum of African American History* (May 1988): 2–3.
6. Levi Coffin, *Reminiscences of Levi Coffin* (Cincinnati: Western Tract Society, 1876), 372.
7. Amy South, "Early Settler's Father Bought Freedom from Half-Brother," *Battle Creek Enquirer News*, 5 May 1974, A-9.
8. Benjamin C. Wilson, *The Rural Black Heritage Between Chicago and Detroit, 1850–1929: A Photograph Album and Random Thoughts* (Kalamazoo: New Issues Press, Western Michigan University, 1985), 37–38.
9. James D. Corrothers, *In Spite of Handicap, An Autobiography* (New York: George H. Doran Co., 1916), 18.

10. Ronald P. Formisano, "The Edge of Caste: Colored Suffrage in Michigan, 1827–1861," *Michigan History Magazine* 56 (Spring 1972): 230.

11. David M. Katzman, "Early Settlers in Michigan," *Michigan Challenge* 8, no. 9 (June 1968): 31.

12. Wilson, *Rural Black Heritage*, 29.

13. Katzman, "Early Settlers in Michigan," 11.

14. Norman K. Miles, "Home at Last: Urbanization of Black Migrants in Michigan, 1916–1929," (Ph.D. diss., University of Michigan, 1978), 49.

15. *Colored Detroit Directory of Business*, 1924. Unpublished.

16. Dan Georgakas and Marvin Surkin, *Detroit: I Do Mind Dying* (New York: St. Martin's Press, 1975), 130.

17. David M. Katzman, "Before the Ghetto: Black Detroit in the Nineteenth Century," (Ph.D. diss., University of Michigan, 1969).

18. Richard W. Thomas, "The Black Self-Help Tradition in Detroit," in *The State of Black Detroit: Building from Strength*, ed. Richard W. Thomas (Detroit: Detroit Urban League, Inc., 1987), 9.

19. Ibid., 10.

20. David M. Katzman, "Rural Blacks in Michigan," *Michigan Challenge*, 9, no. 9 (June 1969): 30.

21. David H. Swinton, "The Economic Status of Black Americans During the 1980s: A Decade of Limited Progress," in *The State of Black America 1990* (New York: National Urban League, Inc., 1990), 25.

22. David Verway, ed., *Michigan Statistical Abstract 1986–87* (Detroit: Wayne State University, Bureau of Business Research, School of Business Administration, 1988), 31–33.

23. John O. Calmore, "National Housing Policies and Black America: Trends, Issues, and Implications" (New York: National Urban League, 1986), 115.

24. James D. McGhee, "The Black Family Today and Tomorrow," in *The State of Black America, 1985* (New York: National Urban League, 1985), 2–8.

25. Frances S. Thomas, "Executive Summary," in *The State of Black Michigan: 1987*, ed. Frances S. Thomas (East Lansing: Urban Affairs Programs, Michigan State University and the Council of Michigan Urban League Executives, 1987), xv.

26. Total Market Data, retrieved 6 September 1998 (*http://www.frasernet .com/mardata.htm*).

27. Clifford L. Broman, "Health of Black Michigan," in *State of Black Michigan: 1987*, 51.

28. Community Health Profile, Kalamazoo County (Michigan), 1997, 29.

29. Clifford L. Broman, "The Health of Black Michigan," in *The State of Black Michigan: 1987*, 51.

30. Paula Farmer, "Detroit Renaissance," *Black Enterprise* 28, no. 11 (June 1998): 234.

31. Bernard E. Anderson, "The Case of Social Policy," in *The State of Black America 1986*, ed. Billy J. Tidwell (New York: National Urban League, 1986), 154.

32. Bonacich, "Racism in Advanced Capitalistic Society," 55.

33. Chester L. Hunt and Lewis Walker, *Ethnic Dynamics: Patterns of Intergroup Relations in Various Societies* (Hohnes Beach, Fla.: Learning Publications, 1974), 359.

Ethnicity in Identity Politics in the Schooling Experiences of African American High School Students

1. Mattias Gardell, "The Sun of Islam Will Rise in the West: Minister Farrakhan and the Nation of Islam in the Latter Days," in *Muslim Communities in North America*, ed. Yvonne Haddad and Jane Smith (Albany: State University of New York Press, 1994), 15–17; Yvonne Haddad and Jane Smith, eds., *Muslim Communities in North America* (Albany: State University of New York Press, 1994), xxiii; and Yvonne Haddad and Jane Smith, *Mission to America: Five Islamic Sectarian Communities in North America* (Gainesville: University of Florida Press, 1993), 87–90.

2. See Wilbur Rich, *Black Mayors and School Politics: The Failure of Reform in Detroit, Gary, and Newark* (New York: Garland, 1996) for a direct comparison of Detroit and Newark black mayoral politics and school reform.

3. Jean Anyon, *Ghetto Schooling: A Political Economy of Urban Educational Reform* (New York: Teachers College Press, 1997).

4. Benjamin Ringer and Elinor Lawless, *Race-Ethnicity and Society* (New York: Routledge, 1989).

5. Jack Glazier, "Issues in Ethnicity," in *Ethnicity in Michigan: Issues and People*, ed. Arthur W. Helweg and Linwood H. Cousins (East Lansing: Michigan State University Press, 2001).

6. Frederik Barth, "Introduction," in *Ethnic Groups and Boundaries: The Social Organization of Culture Difference*, ed. Frederik Barth (London: Allen and Unwin, 1969), 10.

7. Ibid., 14.

8. Ibid., 9–10.

9. Abner Cohen, "Introduction: The Lesson of Ethnicity," in *Urban Ethnicity*, ed. Abner Cohen (London: Tavistock, 1974), xi.

10. Ibid.

11. Manning Nash, *The Cauldron of Ethnicity in the Modern World* (Chicago: University of Chicago Press, 1989).

12. Ronald Cohen, "Ethnicity: Problem and Focus in Anthropology," *Annual Review of Anthropology* 7 (1978): 379–403.

13. Ulf Hannerz, *Soulside: Inquiries into Ghetto Culture and Community* (New York: Columbia University Press, 1969).

14. Penelope Eckert, *Jocks and Burnouts: Social Categories and Identity in the High School* (New York: Teachers College, Columbia University, 1989); Douglas Foley, *Learning Capitalist Culture: Deep in the Heart of Tejas* (Philadelphia: University of Pennsylvania Press, 1990); and Paul Willis, *Learning to Labor: How Working Class Kids Get Working Class Jobs* (New York: Columbia University Press, 1997).

15. Linwood H. Cousins, "'Playing Between Classes': America's Troubles with Class, Race, and Gender in a Black High School and Community," *Anthropology and Education Quarterly* 30, no. 3: 294–315.

16. Signithia Fordham and John Ogbu, "Black Students' School Success: Coping with the Burden of 'Acting White,'" *The Urban Review* 1, no. 3 (1986): 176–206.

17. Signithia Fordham, "Racelessness as a Factor in Black Students' Success: Pragmatic Strategy or Pyrrhic Victory?" *Harvard Educational Review* 58, no. 1 (1988): 54–84.

18. Glazier, "Issues in Ethnicity."

19. For examples of other schools see: Eckert, *Jocks and Burnouts*; Foley, *Learning Capitalist Culture*; Lois Weis and Michelle Fine, eds., *Beyond Silenced Voices: Class, Race, and Gender in United States Schools* (Albany: State University of New York Press, 1993); John Ogbu, *The Next Generation: An Ethnography of Education in an Urban Neighborhood* (New York: Academic Press, 1974) and "Immigrant and Involuntary Minorities in

Comparative Perspective," in *Minority Status and Schooling: A Comparative Study of Immigrant and Involuntary Minorities*, ed. Margaret Gibson and John Ogbu (New York: Garland, 1991); Fordham and Ogbu, "Black Students' School Success"; and Jay MacLeod, *Ain't No Makin' It: Aspirations and Attainment in a Low-Income Neighborhood* (Boulder, Colo.: Westview Press, 1995).

20. Anyon, *Ghetto Schooling*; and Rich, *Black Mayors and School Politics*.

21. C. Eric Lincoln and Lawrence Mamiya, *The Black Church in the African American Experience* (Durham: Duke University Press, 1990).

22. C. Eric Lincoln, *Race, Religion, and the Continuing American Dilemma* (New York: Hill and Wang, 1984), 158.

23. Fordham, "Racelessness as a Factor in Black Students' School Success"; Fordham and Ogbu, *Black Students' School Success*; Ogbu, "Immigrant and Involuntary Minorities in Comparative Perspective;" and John Ogbu, *Minority Education and Caste: The American System in Crosscultural Perspective* (New York: Academic Press, 1978).

24. Henry Giroux, *Border Crossings: Cultural Workers and the Politics of Education* (New York: Routledge, 1992), 180.

25. Michel Foucault, *The Foucault Reader*, ed. Paul Rabinow (New York: Pantheon Books, 1984), 387.

For Further Reference

Books

Anyon, Jean. *Ghetto Schooling: A Political Economy of Urban Educational Reform.* New York: Teachers College Press, Columbia University, 1997.

Barth, Frederik, ed. *Ethnic Groups and Boundaries: The Social Organization of Culture Difference.* London: Allen and Unwin, 1969.

Butchart, Ronald. "'Outthinking and Outflanking the Owners of the World.': A Historiography of the African American Struggle for Education." *History of Education Quarterly* 28, no. 3: 333–66.

Calmore, John O. "National Housing Policies and Black America: Trends, Issues, and Implications." In *The State of Black America, 1986.* New York: National Urban League, 1986.

Cohen, Abner. *Urban Ethnicity.* London: Tavistock, 1974.

Coffin, Levi. *Reminiscences of Levi Coffin.* Cincinnati, Ohio: Western Tract Society, 1876.

Corrothers, James D. *In Spite of Handicap, an Autobiography.* New York: George H. Doran Co., 1916.

Eckert, Penelope. *Jocks and Burnouts: Social Categories and Identity in the High School.* New York: Teachers College, Columbia University, 1989.

Foley, Douglas. *Learning Capitalist Culture: Deep in the Heart of Tejas.* Philadelphia: University of Pennsylvania Press, 1990.

Foucault, Michel. *The Foucault Reader.* Edited by Paul Rabinow. New York: Pantheon Books, 1984.

Franklin, Vincent, and James Anderson, eds. *New Perspectives on Black Educational History.* Boston: G. K. Hall & Co., 1978.

Gardell, Mattias. "The Sun of Islam Will Rise in the West: Minister Farrakhan and the Nation of Islam in the Latter Days." In *Muslim Communities in North America.* Edited by Yvonne Haddad and Jane Smith. Albany: State University of New York Press, 1994.

Georgakas, Dan, and Marvin Surkin. *Detroit: I Do Mind Dying.* New York: St. Martin's Press, 1975.

Gibson, Margaret, and John Ogbu, eds. *Minority Status and Schooling: A Comparative Study of Immigrant and Involuntary Minorities.* New York: Garland, 1991.

Giroux, Henry. *Border Crossings: Cultural Workers and the Politics of Education.* New York: Routledge, 1992.

Haddad, Yvonne, and Jane Smith, eds. *Mission to America: Five Islamic Sectarian Communities in North America.* Gainesville: University of Florida Press, 1993.

———. *Muslim Communities in North America.* Albany: State University of New York Press, 1994.

Hannerz, Ulf. *Soulside: Inquiries into Ghetto Culture and Community.* New York: Columbia University Press, 1969.

Hawkins, Homer, and Richard Thomas, eds. *Blacks and Chicanos in Urban Michigan.* Lansing: History Division, Michigan Department of State, 1979.

Hesslink, George. *Black Neighbors: Negroes in a Northern Rural Community.* Indianapolis, Ind.: Bobbs-Merrill, 1968.

Hunt, Chester L., and Lewis Walker. *Ethnic Dynamics: Patterns of Intergroup Relations in Various Societies.* Hohnes Beach, Fla.: Learned Publications, 1974.

Katzman, David M. *Before the Ghetto: Black Detroit in the Nineteenth Century.* Urbana: University of Illinois Press, 1975.

Lincoln, C. Eric. *Race, Religion, and the Continuing American Dilemma.* New York: Hill and Wang, 1984.

Lincoln, C. Eric, and Lawrence Mamiya. *The Black Church in the African American Experience.* Durham, N.C.: Duke University Press, 1990.

MacLeod, Jay. *Ain't No Makin' It: Aspirations and Attainment in a Low-Income Neighborhood.* Boulder, Colo.: Westview Press, 1995.

Miles, Norman K. "Home at Last: Urbanization of Black Migrants in Detroit, 1916–1929." Ph.D. diss., University of Michigan, 1978.

Nash, Manning. *The Cauldron of Ethnicity in the Modern World.* Chicago: University of Chicago Press, 1989.

Ogbu, John. *Minority Education and Caste: The American System in Crosscultural Perspective.* New York: Academic Press, 1978.

———. *The Next Generation: An Ethnography in an Urban Neighborhood.* New York: Academic Press, 1974.

Rich, Wilbur. *Black Mayors and School Politics: The Failure of Reform in Detroit, Gary, and Newark.* New York: Garland, 1996.

Ringer, Benjamin, and Elinor Lawless. *Race-Ethnicity and Society.* New York: Routledge, 1989.

The State of Black America. New York: National Urban League, 1976.

Thomas, Frances S., ed. *The State of Black Michigan: 1984–1993.* East Lansing: Urban Affairs Program, Michigan State University and the Council of Michigan Urban League Executives, 1987.

Thomas, Richard W. *Life for Us Is What We Make It: Building Black Community in Detroit, 1915–1945.* Bloomington: Indiana University Press, 1992.

———. *The State of Black Detroit: Building from Strength: The Black Self-Help Tradition in Detroit.* Detroit: Detroit Urban League, 1987.

Verway, David, ed. *Michigan Statisical Abstract 1986–87.* Detroit: Wayne State University: Bureau of Business Research, School of Business Administration, 1988.

Weis, Lois, and Michelle Fine, eds. *Beyond Silenced Voices: Class, Race, and Gender in United States Schools.* Albany: State University of New York Press, 1993.

Willis, Paul. *Learning to Labor: How Working Class Kids Get Working Class Jobs.* New York: Columbia University Press, 1997.

Wilson, Benjamin C. "An Epic of Heroism: The Underground Railroad in Michigan, 1837–1870." *Museum of African American History,* May 1988.

———. *The Rural Black Heritage Between Chicago and Detroit, 1850–1929: A Photograph Album and Random Thoughts.* Kalamazoo: New Issues Press, Western Michigan University, 1985.

Wilson, Rosanna. "Biographical Sketch of William Allen of Cass County." Manuscript, n.d., Michigan Historical Collection, Bentley Historical Library, University of Michigan.

Organizations

Black Historic Sites Committee, Michigan Historical Center, Library and Historical Center, 717 West Allegan, Lansing, Michigan 48918; (517) 373-0510

Archives

Benjamin C. Wilson Collection, Department of Black Americana Studies,
Western Michigan University
Michigan Historical Collections, Bentley Historical Library, University of
Michigan
Michigan State Archives, Michigan Historical Center, Lansing, Michigan

Video Resources

Africans in America: America's Journey Through Slavery (Bernice Johnson
Reagon) Boston, Mass. WGBH Educational Foundation, PBS Video, 1998.
Videocassette. DVD.

Museums

Second Baptist Church, 441 Monroe St., Detroit, Michigan 48226; (313) 895-7322
Charles H. Wright Museum of African American History, 315 E. Warren, Detroit,
Michigan 48201-1443; (313) 494-5800
Your Heritage House, 110 East Ferry, Detroit, Michigan 48202; (313) 871-1667
Idlewild Cultural Museum, 5583 Broadway Ave., Idlewild, Michigan 49642; (231)
745-7541

Important Historic Sites

Nathan Macy Thomas House (Schoolcraft)
Undergound Railroad Sculpture (Battle Creek)
Sojourner Truth Sculpture Site (Calhoun County)
Sojourner Truth Grave Site (Calhoun County)
Underground Railroad Marker (Cass County)
Chain Lake Missionary Baptist (Cass County)

Idlewild Resort (Lake County)

Laura Haviland Statue (Lenawee County)

Old Settlers Picnic Grounds (Mecosta County)

Woodland Park (Newaygo County)

Frederick Douglass and John Brown Meeting Marker (Wayne County)

Ossian Sweet Home (Wayne County)

National Museum of the Tuskegee Airmen (Wayne County)

Crispus Attucks American Legion #59 (Kent County)

Enoch Harris Family Marker (Kalamazoo County)

Eagle Lake Resort (Van Buren County)

Index

A

Africa, 4, 15
Alexander, L. P., 6
Allen, Norman, 6
Archer, Dennis, 28
Atlee, Dr. E. A., 6

B

Barnes, Charles, 6
Battle Creek, 11, 14, 15, 16
Beckley, Guy, 6
Benton Harbor, 2, 16
Berrien County, 6
Berrys, 15
Black Muslim Movement, 31
Bogue, Stephen, 6
Bracys, 15
Bradley, Robert, 10
Buckner, Ruth Owens, 16

C

Cabin Creek, 11
Caldwell, John, 6

Cass County, 6, 16
Chadwick, Theron, Sr., 6
Chrysler, 28
Coffin Levi, 6
Cole, William, 10
Community High, 36, 38, 44
Cox and Campbell, Drs., 6
Cross, Thomas, 15
Cushman, Henry J., 6

D

Davis, Norm, 19
DeBaptiste, George, 6
Densmore, Abel, 6
Detroit, 4, 6, 16, 17, 18, 23, 24, 33
Detroit Public Schools, 33
Dexter, Samuel W., 6
Drake County (Ohio), 14
Dodge, Silas, 6

E

Evergreen Valley, 19

F

Farad, W. D., 31
Finney, Seymour, 7
Flint, 16, 19
Ford, Henry, 18, 28
Foster, Theodore, 6

G

Geddes, John, 6
General Motors, 18, 28
Genessee County, 15
Gidley, Townsend E., 6
Graves, Helen Hill, 17
Greenville Creek, 12
Greenville Valley, 14
Grifens, James, 10

H

Hampton, Wade, 10
Henderson, Thomas, 6
Hussey, Erastus, 6
Humphrey, Rev. Luther, 6
Indiana, 11, 14
Harris, Albert, 16
Harris, Minerva Wright, 16
Hicksites, 6
Humphrey, Rev. Luther, 6
Hussey, Erastus, 9

I

Idlewild, 2
Isabella County, 15

J

Johnson, Frances, 10

K

Kalamazoo, 15, 16

L

Lambert, William, 6
Lane, Abraham, 10

Lee, Ishmael, 6
Logan County (Ohio), 14
Logan Street/Martin Luther King
       Boulevard (Lansing, Mich.), 25

M

Malleable Iron Company, 16
McCullon, William, 6
McIlvain, E., 6
Mecosta County, 15
Mercer County (Ohio), 14
Michilimackinac, 4
Michigan Manual of Freemen's
       Progress, 21
Mills, Mary, 10
Monroe County, 6
Montague, Henry, 6
Montcalm County, 15
Muslim, 41

N

Nation of Islam, 31, 40, 41
Newark (New Jersey), 2, 31, 35, 42
Nicholas, Samuel, 6

O

Ohio, 12, 14
Ontario, Canada, 15
Osborn, Josiah, 6
Owens, 15
Owens, Martin, 16

Q

Quakers, 6, 7
Quinn Chapel A. M. E. Church, 16

R

Randolph County (Indiana), 14
Rawson, August, 6
Roberts family, 20
Roberts, Willis, 20
"Run, Nigger, Run," 7

S

Second Baptist Church
(Kalamazoo), 22
Shelby County (Indiana), 14
Shelby County (Ohio), 14
Shugart, Zacharian, 6
Silverdome, 25
Snow, Orrin, 6
Stevens, Rev. A., 10
Strauther, Samuel, 6

T

Thayer, S. B., 6
Thomas, Dr. Nathan Macy, 6
Tone, Peter, 10

Truth, Sojourner, 15

U

Underground Railroad, 4, 7, 8
University of Michigan, 26

W

Washington, Julia, 10
Wayne County (Indiana), 14
Webb, William, 6
Wesley, John, 10
Wheeler, Dr. William, 6
Wheelers, Charles, 6
Wilson, Albert, 10